Accounting for Beginners 2023

The Ultimate Guide to Grow Your Business with Simple Accounting Practices and Smart Bookkeeping Strategies to Reach the Next Level

Roger Myers

Table of Contents

INTRODUCTION

Almost every business relies on its bookkeepers. If you believe that information is valuable, you will see the importance of a bookkeeper in a firm. The information included in books helps business owners to manage a variety of financial aspects of their firm while also making critical decisions such as market strategy or product launches.

Without the ongoing labor of bookkeepers, most businesses would have little understanding of their financial status. Without particular financial knowledge, the business executive would only be speculating on the number of sales made, cash taken and withdrawn, cash paid out, and items sold to clients during the year. It would be impossible to ascertain how much was spent on other firm essentials or on salaries for our employees.

Every firm and people who work inside it require dependable and correct financial documentation. Executives, title-holders, staffs, and external teams like stockholders, financiers, and government officials rely heavily on the accountant to appropriately record financial dealings.

If you are an employee who keeps the books for a small business owner or a business owner who handles the finances yourself, your position is crucial, and you must learn accounting principles. Bookkeepers need to be meticulous, love dealing with numbers, and be careful to enter data into records accurately.

However, if you are new to the subject, you may find these steps difficult to follow at first - so we've put together an easy-to-follow guide on how to get started.

What You Can Get from This Book

Bookkeeping is an ongoing process that starts with financial transactions. This book will walk you through;

- Journal entries for such transactions
- A global ledger is updated with those transactions

- Making sure your books are balanced by checking them
- Making the required adjustments or modifications
- Making financial reporting more readable and effective

Who is this book for?

I'd presume one of two things if you chose to read this book in order to gain explicit information.

- A company owner who desires to get knowledge in bookkeeping. You most likely have a fundamental grasp of the market and its jargon, but little familiarity with bookkeeping and accounting.
- A person who has previously studied bookkeeping and is looking for a comprehensive review or reference work.
- A representative of a private venture who has as of late been approached to assume control over the accounting liabilities should grasp precisely the way in which exchanges are accounted for in the books. They should likewise comprehend how to guarantee that the passages are made accurately and precisely, and how to report monetary data utilizing the information assembled.
- a person interested in learning more about how to organize and maintain records who now does bookkeeping for a small business or who hopes to do so. You likely understand a few businesses' lingo, but you have no knowledge of accounting or bookkeeping. As an alternative, possibly lastly.
- A person who is transitioning into a new job or capacity where accounting and bookkeeping skills are essential.

Using an accountant is the most cost-effective way to file your taxes. It's just a little more work than filing without an accountant, but you're going to save a good amount of time and money over time. Don't go for the cheapest option. Any accountant will tell you that they get a lot of calls from people asking for price comparisons.

CHAPTER 1:
Bookkeeping Basics

Most entrepreneurs use bookkeepers to work for their benefit. Also, think about what else? The cost can frequently be restrictive for an independent venture; in this way, the proprietor utilizes a clerk to act as the bookkeeper's eyes and ears. The bookkeeper consistently surveys the clerk's work and assists them with laying out sound accounting methods. Each entrepreneur needs to save costs while expanding income and dealing with your own books might assist you with doing that.

Figuring out accounting

The organization and upkeep of monetary records, for example, records, budget summaries, annual duty records, and so on, is known as accounting. The bookkeeping system known as accounting frequently alluded to as record-keeping, monitors buys, costs, and other business processes in the bookkeeping framework. The information assembled by means of accounting is utilized to deliver budget summaries. Accounting is the method involved with contributing information to a bookkeeping framework or put it another way. A paper record might be utilized for this physically, or you can do it carefully with bookkeeping programs like QuickBooks, Sage, and Xero, to give some examples. In spite of the way that accounting has various advantages, many individuals secure the position to be troublesome, exhausting and scorned.

The job of a clerk

The clerk is responsible for observing the monetary action of a business in its books. Most of the accountants to a great extent depend on cheap innovation to deal with and orchestrate information. The fundamental obligations of a clerk change contingent upon the size and sort of business.

Accounting Task

Basically, bookkeeping contains recording and keeping up with track of information that is straightforwardly pertinent to an association's monetary circumstance. It is fundamental for both enormous and independent companies, however, what does it really involve? A few parts of bookkeeping incorporate the accompanying:

1. Revenue and costs caused by a business are followed through accounting. One of the most critical (and tedious) parts of accounting is monitoring business pay and expenses since it frames the reason for any remaining accounting and bookkeeping methodology. As a result of the significance of this data and the chance of human blunder, most organizations use mechanized bookkeeping frameworks to limit how much manual following is required.

2. Upkeep of the overall record: An overall business record goes about as the establishment of the information assortment process utilized by bookkeepers, saving and sorting out the monetary information expected to create budget reports for the association. It is comprised of a sub-record that might hold quite a few diaries.

3. Accounts payable alludes to the amounts of cash owing by your business to providers, makers, state-run administrations, and different elements, though debt claims allude to the amounts of cash owed by your clients for the items or administrations they have bought.

4. Managing bank compromise: It is an unavoidable piece of bookkeeping that there are events when the detailed exchange is not really affirmed by the ledgers. Compromise is expected in these circumstances, which contains contrasting bank articulations with accounting archives and distinguishing the reason for any disparities. On the off chance that you wind up in this situation, make an effort not to stress excessively; assuming you know what to do, nothing remains to be stressed over.

5. Providing fiscal summaries: As was at that point said, accounting requires the formation of the accompanying budget reports:

    a. A monetary record principally fills in as a report on an organization's monetary standing. It basically records the resources, liabilities, and value of the owner(s) starting around a specific date. Just communicated, the accounting report shows the organization's net worth.

    b. The pay explanation, once in a while alluded to as the benefit and shortfall proclamation is an administration report for an organization that rundowns deals, expenses, and a net gain for a specific time frame period.

    c. Statement of Cash Flow: Cash is the top dog. An income proclamation shows how cash is gotten and spent over a specific timeframe. Considering that it uncovers how much cash you genuinely make, this is maybe one of the main markers for an entrepreneur.

    d. The Statement of Changes in Equity is a component of each and every organization's yearly investor report, and it is arranged every year. This way, it's anything but an expected piece of the month-to-month fiscal report. This assertion looks at the value of a partnership throughout a bookkeeping period.

Why Accounting is Significant

Accounting, or the proper documentation and coordinating of a partnership's monetary exercises, is essential to any activity's monetary practicality, particularly that of an entrepreneur. A strong handle on money empowers entrepreneurs to make sound suppositions and diminishes the gamble of money misappropriation. Accounting is inseparably attached to the production of budget reports, income to the board, and duty implementation; viable accounting offers a strong starting point for translation and verification with the rest. Coming up next are the absolute most huge advantages of bookkeeping, which might make sense of why it is the most sought-after expertise in private companies.

1. Professional Documentation: A conscientious and dedicated clerk will continuously keep exact and nitty-gritty records. This broad documentation aids the monetary organization of your association. Since the data is as of now set up, it is incredibly significant in the event that your fiscal summaries are required, or the business is evaluated.

2. Bookkeeping Gives Crucial Data About the General Strength of a Business: Accounting assists organizations with making fiscal reports that incorporate monetary data as well as a concise portrayal of how the business is doing. The reports empower you to screen the organization's money inflows and surges (the money that streams into the business and leaves the business at some random time). This is known as an organization's income. Assessed incomes are fundamental for drawing in new financial backers and ensuring current ones. Realizing your organization's monetary achievement makes it simpler to anticipate enlisting development and everyday activities. Budget reports, for example, your monetary record, give fundamental data that empowers you to go with key business decisions equitably instead of quickly.

3. Bookkeeping Guides in Duty Readiness: When expense season starts, and you want to give your bookkeeper the fundamental archives to report corporate assessments, keeping proper records diminishes how much time is expected to finish up these tax documents emphatically. As opposed to searching through your organization records, the bookkeeper will zero in on distinguishing qualified charge exceptions, setting aside your time and cash.

4. Tax Evaluations: Expense appraisals are utilized to lay out how much assessment is attributable to the administrative and nearby legislatures. An expense report must be finished on the off chance that all monetary exchanges have been gotten. Effective bookkeeping might help firms in keeping their assessment issues altogether and deciding the genuine measure of expense payable. The data expected in expense forms should be right and full. The inability to keep charge records current might bring about extreme results like critical fines and claims. To keep away from punishments and claims, bookkeeping is pivotal in giving the right information in a top-notch style and on time.

5. Bookkeeping limits the effect of a review: Organizations might be examined eventually. It's not something worth talking about to anticipating, however it merits getting ready for. Having your books coordinated and in one area simplifies it by introducing monetary data at the appropriate time, which can assist you with staying away from fines or over-the-top punishments.

Single-Passage versus Twofold Section Accounting

With regard to accounting, you should choose between single-passage and twofold section bookkeeping. This is an issue that numerous entrepreneurs defy, especially individuals who don't have a lot of skill with accounting and wish to deal with their own records. Under single-section bookkeeping, all corporate activities are kept in a solitary record. Due to the fact that it is so easy to run; this is the manner by which new organizations start. In the twofold section of bookkeeping, every exchange is recorded as two exchanges, with the complete details as 'charge' and 'credit.' These presentations where your cash is coming from and where it is going. Albeit twofold section, bookkeeping takes additional time, it gives a more far-reaching image of an organization's monetary information.

Fundamental Stage of Accounting

Accounting might be a difficult strategy on occasion, yet understanding an intelligent series of steps will simplify it. Some accounting tasks are as per the following:

a. Source Report Planning: The source records act as the establishment for all accounting tasks. At the point when an organization submits a request for an item, the producer will give it a deal's receipt. At the point when an organization gets cash from a bank, it signs a promissory note, which it keeps a duplicate of. At the point when a purchaser arranges an item or administration utilizing a Mastercard, the firm saves the Visa slip as verification of the deal. Every one of these business structures fills in as an unavoidable wellspring of data in any bookkeeping procedure; at the end of the day, they are basic pieces that the clerk uses to record the monetary effect of the organization's activities.

b. Documenting the Monetary Ramifications of Business Action in Source Records: Deals and buys (Exchanges) have monetary results that should be reported; their culmination decides if the business is in an ideal situation, more regrettable off, or "unconcerned." Other business exercises that affect the firm incorporate employing a new workforce, making retail buys, getting cash from a bank, and buying direct-selling items. The bookkeeping system begins with recognizing the significant data for every exchange. The Main Bookkeeper of the association creates rules and philosophies for estimating the monetary results of these exchanges. Practically certain, the accountant will comply to determined guidelines and methods.

c. Original Monetary Exchange Passages: The clerk embeds the initial sections into the diary and afterward into the organization accounts utilizing the source document(s) for every exchange. A diary is a deliberate record of occasions in the request wherein they happened. A record is a discrete record relating to a particular sort of business movement. A solitary exchange influences at least two records. While recording an exchange, it is important to utilize the organization's laid-out chart(s) of records.

d. End-of-period activities are fundamental for keeping up with current bookkeeping documentation and making them accessible for the recording of the board bookkeeping reports, expense forms, and fiscal summaries.

e. Compiling the Changed Preliminary Equilibrium for the Bookkeeper: Following the fruition of all finish-of-period exercises, the clerk readies an intensive breakdown, all things considered, regularly alluded to as the changed preliminary equilibrium. Little and medium-sized organizations oversee many records for resources, liabilities, value, income, and expenses. Bigger organizations can have huge numbers of records, while enormous associations can keep several thousand. Charge reports, outside fiscal summaries, and interior bookkeeping notes to chiefs, then again, contain a couple of records. The typical outer monetary record, for instance, incorporates only 25 to thirty records (perhaps less), while the ordinary personal government form has an insignificant number of records. The bookkeeping official will consolidate the redressed preliminary offset with the relevant records to create a synopsis figure that will be remembered for the fiscal summaries or duty filings. A company, for instance, may have many different stock records, every one of which is reflected in the changed preliminary equilibrium. The bookkeeper joins these records into a solitary outline stock report, which is then remembered as the organization's true asset report. The bookkeeping official will sort the records as per expressed monetary revealing norms and annual duty arrangements.

f. Closing the Books: All far-reaching sets of organization bookkeeping are alluded to as "books." A deal is a ceaseless series of occasions that impacts the production of yearly explanations and expense forms. By shutting the books for the year and beginning once more for the next year, the business will actually want to make an unmistakable differentiation between the tasks of the equitable finished year (generally a year bookkeeping period) and the previous year.

CHAPTER 2: Basics of Accounting

The most vital phase in turning into a splendid bookkeeping master is grasping the basics of bookkeeping. As you go through your bookkeeping profession, you will discover that all that returns to the rudiments. All modern bookkeeping computations and cycles are based on the basics, and you will as often as possible use this information to create last reports and survey what they demonstrate. Therefore, I suggest that you give close consideration.

Bookkeeping Standards

Bookkeeping standards are wide norms that affect and control the bookkeeping area. These standards give the setting inside which data given by different bookkeeping frameworks becomes reliable, pertinent, and important. Among the significant bookkeeping ideas are:

1. Accrual's standard. This is the most key reason, and it includes the keep and ID of income in the monetary records when it is acquired as opposed to when it is gotten in real money. Costs should likewise be reported when they are brought about, not when they are paid, as per the standard. Fiscal reports can be produced on a gathering premise under sound accounting guidelines (GAAP), allowing the standard.

2. Going concern rule. This idea expresses that those organizations ought to be treated like they will be in activity endlessly. Thus, the thought proposes that the business/venture has no aim of shutting or selling and will keep on working soon.

3. Time period guideline. This guideline stresses the need of representing an organization's prosperity at one point in time, despite the fact that the exercises are wanted to everlastingly proceed.

4. Historical expense standard. This idea expresses that accounting report resources ought to be recorded at the worth at which they were bought, i.e., the price tag, as opposed to the market worth of the thing at that point.

5. Accounting element guideline. As per this thought, the business and its proprietors are two distinct legitimate substances. Productivity is frequently appointed to the firm, while the proprietor endeavors to create benefits from exercises. Subsequently, their targets are exceptional and particular.

6. Full revelation rule. The idea commands that all exchanges or things that might affect the fiscal summaries be completely revealed. Since an outcome, an organization shouldn't smother any data relating to the organization, as this might overallly affect the independent direction.

7. Matching Rule. This idea orders that firm costs be kept in a similar period as the going with incomes were gathered. This hypothesis supports the detailing of an organization's benefit throughout a particular time span. Genuine is not set in stone by complying with this rule.

8. Monetary unit guideline. This thought is established with the understanding that the main deals that might be conveyed are those that can be communicated in financial units.

Therefore, non-quantifiable things, for example, skill level and client assistance quality can't be archived.

9. Realization rule. This thought expresses that pay must be recorded when the hidden administrations and items have been performed or conveyed. Just said, income should be created in its entirety before it very well may be recorded.

10. Conservatism idea. This thought advocate objectivity and decency. When stood up with two choices, the thought directs that the one with the least returns be accounted for. Accordingly, in the event that two resources have similar returns, the one with the lesser return ought to be expressed. Subsequently, with regard to liabilities, the one with the biggest worth ought to be revealed.

11. Consistency idea. This idea depends on the reason that chose bookkeeping principles and methods should be utilized reliably across the course of tasks. Therefore, it is against proceeding to adjust approaches or procedures until significant.

12. Materiality idea. As indicated by the hypothesis, data and material are respected to be huge on the off chance that they affect a sensible individual's perspective or assessment. Subsequently, every data that is expected to essentially affect the fiscal reports is considered significant and should be enough proclaimed and perceived.

13. Neutrality idea. This thought advances objectivity, particularly with respect to inspectors and bookkeepers while getting ready monetary records. Indeed, even while bookkeepers might want to see benefits in the different organizations where they work, they should stay unprejudiced and give current realities as they are.

CHAPTER 3: Accounting Terminologies

Presently, the time has come to familiarize ourselves with the wordings utilized in bookkeeping. This section can be utilized as a word reference of bookkeeping.

Bookkeeper:

A bookkeeper is an individual who is responsible for bookkeeping. He is an authority responsible for the association's bookkeeping capability. A Sanctioned Bookkeeper is a monetary bookkeeping proficient (CA).

Bookkeeping:

"Bookkeeping is a craft of recording, ordering, and summing up in a critical way and concerning cash, exchanges, and occasions that are, to some extent, basically of a monetary person, and deciphering the outcomes thereof," as per the American Organization of Guaranteed Public Bookkeepers (AICPA).

Clients of Bookkeeping Data:

1. Management requires convenient data for arranging, controlling, and navigation. Proprietors and Investors

2. Investors, clients, contenders, stock trades, state-run administrations, and expense specialists are instances of outer clients.

Accounting:

It is the workmanship and study of recording the money-related part of business and monetary exchanges in books of record.

Two frameworks of accounting are:

1. Single passage arrangement of accounting.

2. Double-passage arrangement of accounting.

Two premises or frameworks of bookkeeping are:

1. Cash Premise and

2. Mercantile (Accumulation) Premise

Books of Records:

The Books of Records record an organization all's monetary exchanges. The Diary Book and the Record Book are the two primary Books of Records.

Diary: is a book of driving sections wherein all monetary exchanges for the year are reported in sequential request, i.e., by date, by passing diary passages. The diary might be separated into nine diary volumes.

Sub-division of Diary Books:

Enormous companies, specifically, as to separate the Diary into nine segments. They are as per the following:

1. Purchase Book - to record credit acquisition of things for exchanging, Deals Book - to record credit deals of items for exchange.

2. Purchase Returns Book - used to record returns of bought items that were blemished or undervalued.

3. Sales Returns Book - Used to record the arrival of offered items because of harm or different causes.

4. Cash Book - A book used to record money or bank exchanges utilizing cash receipts, really take a look at counter thwarts, vouchers, etc.

5. Petty Money Book - Used to monitor small money installments and strange little receipts in light of vouchers.

6. Bills Receivable Book - Used to monitor bills or promissory notes given by debt holders.

7. Bills Payable Book - To record bills or promissory notes given to leasers;

8. Journal Appropriate. - To record rectification of blunder passages, moving sections, opening sections, shutting sections, Changing sections, etc.

Account:

A record is a united portrayal of all exchanges connected with that record. Account is shortened as (a/c).

Charge (Dr) and Credit (Cr):

They address different sides of a story. In a "T" record, a/c Dr is on the left and Cr is on the right. When journalizing an exchange, one should choose whether the a/c ought to be Dr or Cr by following the Journalizing standards of Dr and Cr.

Record

This is a book that contains various records relating to the proprietors' capital, the proprietors' withdrawal i.e., drawings, individual records of Various Debt holders (S Drs), Various Lenders (S Crs), resources, properties, Bills Receivable (B/R), cash, Bank, Bills Payable (B/P), Credit liabilities, stock, a load of merchandise, etc. Leger is alluded to as a beneficial book.

Sub-division of Record Book:

A major business record book might be isolated into three segments as follows:

1. Debtors or Deals record,
2. Creditors or Buy Record,
3. The general record contains resources, liabilities, capital or value, income, and expenses.

Record Posting:

It is the method involved with contributing diary passage data to the proper record accounts. The record charged (Dr) is set apart with "To credited account data" on the charge side, while the record acknowledged (Cr) is set apart with "By charged account data" on the credit side.

Adjusting of Record:

All record accounts are adjusted consistently. The money book, then again, is adjusted consistently. Adjusting a record involves having the best all out in the first situation on both the Dr and Cr sides. Then register the contrast between the Dr absolute and the Cr all out. Assuming Dr is more than Cr (for example Dr > Cr), the equilibrium is a charge; embed the distinction on the acknowledged side as "By Equilibrium c/d (conveyed down)". Assuming Cr is more than Dr (for example Cr > Dr), it is a credit balance; the distinction ought to be recorded on the charge side as "To Adjust c/d (conveyed down)". The earlier day's end balance turns into the following day's starting equilibrium. The completion balance set apart as "By Equilibrium c/d (conveying down)" turns into the beginning offset the following day with the passage "To Adjust b/d (cut down)". The closure balance set apart as "To Adjust c/d (conveyed down)" turns into the beginning offset the following day with the passage "By Equilibrium b/d (cut down)".

Conveyed forward:

It is the methodology of taking the end balance sum at the record end or foot of the page, which is abridged as c/f (Conveyed forward) or c/d (Conveyed down).

Presented:

It is the most common way of bringing the sum toward the start of the record or from the finish of the past page to the highest point of the accompanying page forward. The shortening is b/f (Presented) or b/d (Cut down).

Bookkeeping year:

The records are made for a year. By and large, in USA bookkeeping year begins from first October and closures on 30th September of each and every year, which is called monetary year. In Europe schedule year (first January to 31st December) while in UK the year begins from sixth April and closures on fifth April of each and every year.

Merchandise:

The expression "merchandise" alludes to all products, things, or things obtained for resale. We partition the products account into five segments for the end goal of bookkeeping:

1. Sales a/c,
2. Sales Returns or Return inwards a/c,
3. Purchase a/c,
4. Purchase Returns or Return outward a/c,
5. Stock a/c.

Buy:

Buys incorporate any articles, items, or items bought for resale, whether paid in real money or on layaway. Buys are ordinarily traded items.

Deals:

Deals incorporate any items, wares, or items that are broadly exchanged merchandise and are traded for money or credit.

Buy Returns or Get back outward:

At the point when procured items are broken, poor, unsatisfactory, or mistakenly provided, they are gotten back to the source or merchant, and there is an outward return. A purchase return happens to fix a charging botch, surpassing charging than the concurred rate. A charge Note is a record given to the merchant to bring things back.

Deals Returns or Get back internal:

At the point when sold items are flawed, inadmissible, unsatisfactory, or inaccurately conveyed, the client returns them; this is known as getting back internal. At the point when there is a blunder in invoicing, for example, charging for more than the concurred sum, a deals discount ends up fixing it. A Credit Note is a record given to the client for bringing things back.

Stock:

Stock alludes to items procured available to be purchased yet not sold starting around a particular date. Stock alludes to items gained for assembling however not used or fabricated yet not sold. In this way, there may be a load of completed things, stock of natural substances, or supply of semi-completed merchandise or work underway. Stock is a transient Current resource for the organization that is demonstrated in the B/S.

Voucher:

A voucher is a record that fills in as documentation or confirmation of a business exchange. A money voucher is a typical structure for recording negligible money installments. A voucher is a composed report that fills in as the establishment for the organization's bookkeeping records. A voucher is a little printed piece of paper that might be reclaimed for items or administrations or qualifies the conveyor for a rebate.

Receipt:

A receipt is a composed business report given by the vendor to a purchaser. It contains data on the offer of labor and products, including charges. The receipt is outward (for example outward receipt) for the dealer, though the indistinguishable receipt is internal for the purchaser (for example internal receipt). The documentation verification for a business exchange is the outward receipt (created by us). The internal receipt (delivered by the dealer) fills in as narrative documentation of the buying exchange.

Account holders (Drs):

An indebted person is somebody who owes cash to an organization for buying labor and products using a credit card. On the resource side of the financial record, debt holders are identified as Drs.

Lenders (Crs):

A lender is an individual who is owed cash by the firm. At the point when another individual gives items, administrations, or benefits to a business on layaway, the total owed to that individual addresses the bank. On the risk side of the Financial record, loan bosses are meant as Crs.

Charge Note:

This is a record given by the client to the vendor for the arrival of gained things. The charge note provided by us fills in as archived confirmation for the buy bring exchange back.

Credit Note:

This is a report given by the merchant to the client for the arrival of sold things. The credit note provided by the merchant fills in as formal confirmation of the event of the deals to bring the exchange back.

Rebate:

Limiting is the decrease in the worth of deals. There are two sorts of limits: exchange limits and money limits. The expression "exchange markdown" alludes to a decrease in the selling cost. Therefore, it isn't perceived as an exchange as isn't kept in bookkeeping. Cash Markdown is a decline in the sum inferable from business, which is subsequently monetary in nature and is reflected in bookkeeping.

Contra section:

Contra section happens when a money book is kept up within a few segments, like Money and Bank (for example twofold segment) or Money, Bank, and Money Rebate (for example triple section), under the diary framework sub-division. Since the Money Book is both a diary and a record account, the J/F and L/F are something similar. All the while, there is a ledger in total agreement that requires a J/F reference. At the point when both record accounts (Money a/c and Bank a/c) show in total agreement next to each other, there is a counter passage situation. Since references to diary folio (J/F) and record folio (L/F) occur in a similar region, rather than composing J/F number and L/F number, basically letter "C" is utilized to demonstrate contra passage. At the point when an exchange influences both the Money and Financial balances, a contra passage happens. At the point when money is put into or removed from a financial balance, a counter section is made in the Money Book.

Preliminary Equilibrium:

It is a gathering explanation for all record account adjustments, whether Dr or Cr, on a particular day. It is intended to evaluate the numerical rightness of bookkeeping since the Dr side all out should rise to the Cr side aggregate. Dr = Cr in a twofold passage accounting framework. On the off chance that the Dr aggregate and Cr absolute are not indistinguishable, it recommends that there is an issue that must be rectified prior to getting ready budget reports.

Budget reports:

An organization element's budget reports, which incorporate Assembling, Exchanging, and Benefit and Misfortune accounts, as well as the Monetary record, are ready at the finish of the financial year. Be that as it may, fiscal summaries including pay and use a/c and the monetary record are made for non-benefit associations or experts.

Producing a/c:

This a/c is produced when there is an assembling business. All assembling costs are displayed on the Dr side, while assembling pay is accounted for on the Cr side.

Exchanging a/c:

This a/c is made when there is an exchange business. All expenses related to buying are accounted for on the Dr side, while deals and shutting stocks are accounted for on the Cr side. This record's equilibrium is either net benefit or gross deficit.

P and L a/c (Benefit and Misfortune a/c):

All aberrant consumptions related to buying, assembling, and selling are recorded on the Dr side, though roundabout pay and incomes are recorded on the Cr side. This record's equilibrium is either net benefit or overall deficit, and it is conveyed to the Asset report.

Pay and Use a/c:

This record is opened by a non-exchanging body, for example, Experts or a non-benefit association like Clubs, NGO, SGH, or AOP. This record's equilibrium is either Excess or Deficiency, and it is conveyed to the Asset report.

Benefit:

Is characterized as the abundance of incomes over related expenses or costs; subsequently, Benefit = Income - Use.

Misfortune:

It is characterized as an overabundance of expenses or costs above pay. Thus, Misfortune = Consumption - Income.

Monetary record (B/S):

Is an assertion of resources, liabilities, and capital starting around a particular date. It shows what is going on. It is either a business depiction or a X-beam. Because of the comprehension of dualities, a B/S should adjust. Accordingly, Resources = Liabilities + Capital.

Capital:

is the sum contributed by the entrepreneurs. Capital demonstrates the proprietor's case or part of the organization's resources. According to Accounting report the condition: {Capital = Resources - Liabilities}.

Drawings:

is how much money, items, or other resource are eliminated by the entrepreneur for individual or homegrown use. Drawings mirror a decrease in the proprietor's case or piece of the business' resources. Drawings are much of the time reflected in the B/S as a derivation from Capital a/c.

Resources:

these are the resources or assets that the corporate element possesses. Cash, furniture, plant and apparatus, stock or stock, altruism, B/R, bank stores, etc are models. Resources are named; Fixed

Resources, which might be Substantial fixed resources Theoretical fixed resources, and Current Resources

Fixed resources:

are properties and items used to produce income. They are not instantly available for purchase.

Substantial fixed resources:

Substantial resources are those that should be visible and contacted. model: Speculations, Furniture, and Apparatuses, Gear.

Theoretical resources:

Theoretical resources are resources that shouldn't be visible or contacted, like generosity, brand names, licenses, and duplicate freedoms.

Generosity:

is an immaterial resource that addresses the worth of the association's name, notoriety, and notoriety? It is esteemed right now of an adjustment of business proprietorship, like the acknowledgment of another accomplice or a corporate consolidation.

Current Resources:

These resources vary frequently in something like a year, and there is either stream or current. Cash accounts, stock, Various Debt holders (S Drs), Bills Receivables (B/R), Costs paid ahead of time, Pay acquired however not got, etc are models.

Charges Receivables (B/R):

It is a responsibility from the indebted individuals that installment will be made on the due day.

Costs paid advance:

Any expenses paid for a period that reaches out over the monetary year are viewed as abundance paid ahead of time. At the point when pay rates are paid for quite a long time, the initial three months are named advance pay.

Livelihoods procured yet not got:

is the term for Accumulated Pay. At the point when a decent store is made in a bank, premium is paid by the details of the bank. This will bring about a circumstance where premium is procured however not got, frequently known as Gathered Interest.

Liabilities:

are the corporate element's commitments owed to different gatherings. Fixed and current liabilities are both conceivable.

Fixed Liabilities:

Fixed liabilities are long haul commitments that should be paid. Capital, Value Offer, Inclination Offer, Bank Credit, Home loans, Debentures, and Bonds are a few models.

Current Risk:

These are commitments that should be met in a brief timeframe, ideally soon. Various lenders (S Crs), bills payable (B/P), bank over draft (Body), exceptional expenses, income got ahead of time, etc are instances of current liabilities.

Charges Payables (B/P):

It is a responsibility made by the organization to its loan bosses that installment will be made on time.

Extraordinary Costs (O/s Costs):

They are costs brought about yet not paid all through the monetary year. For instance, on the off chance that a staff part's compensation is paid for a very long time, one month's pay is owed for the twelfth month.

Salaries got ahead of time:

At the point when cash is gotten ahead of time, it isn't created inside the monetary year. Lease got for a long time incorporates one month's lease got ahead of time.

Bank Compromise Articulation (BRS):

We hold ledgers in business. Essentially, the bank stores our i.e., client a/c in its book, and a copy of the equivalent is given to the business as a Pass Book. Sooner or later, the bank balance in our books ought to match the bank balance in the Pass Book. It doesn't necessarily work out. Thus, a Bank Compromise Explanation (BRS) itemizing the purposes behind the debate is required.

Bookkeeping Blunders:

Committing errors is regular. Records might be composed mistakenly. Blunders should be revised utilizing amendment diary sections.

Moving Passages:

In bookkeeping, there are times when the equilibrium of one record is moved to one more by utilizing a moving passage. Models incorporate moving net benefit from Exchanging a/c to P& L a/c and drawing's a/c to Capital a/c.

Changing Sections:

While utilizing a trade bookkeeping framework, it is expected to change sections. Thus, advance or exceptional expenses, cash got ahead of time or pay created yet not got, and different things should be adjusted. An end stock changing passage is likewise vital.

Shutting Passages:

To evaluate benefit or misfortune at the finish of the monetary year, all ostensible records should be shut. To close the pay rates account, the information is P&L a/c Dr to Pay rates a/c.

Opening Passages:

To open records for the following year an initial diary passage must be passed. It is intricate or compound passage Dr all resources and Cr all Liabilities and Capital a/cs.

Journal

Date	Particulars	L/F	Dr Amount	Cr Amount
01-04-2022	Furniture a/c Dr		20,000	
	S.Drs -Richmond School a/cDr		8,000	
	Closing Stock a/c Dr		7,200	
	Indian Bank a/c Dr		36,000	
	Cash a/c Dr		51,400	
	To S Crs = Oriental Fan a/c			20,000
	To Capital a/c			1,02,600
	(Being opening journal entry for the new year, capital being difference amount of Dr & Cr which is equal to Capital a/c bal c/d)			

Dissolvable:

is an individual whose resources are more than that of his liabilities.

A ruined:

is an individual whose resources are not adequate to meet the installment of his liabilities in full.

CHAPTER 4:
What's New in Bookkeeping for Small Business?

Accounting is continuously advancing, and new programming is continually being delivered. We should investigate a portion of the methodologies and programming applications accessible to you as a little organization proprietor.

Open a Business Ledger

You maintain that your organization should find true success. Nonetheless, how might you keep up with your own assets, particularly from your business funds? The arrangement is direct: make an organization ledger.

At the point when you blend your business income and expenses with your own pay and spending, it is extremely challenging to evaluate how your firm is performing. To find out whether your bank has a business account open, check with them first.

Choose the Best Accounting Software for Your Company

You will require a record or a cashbook in any event. The cashbook might be essentially finished utilizing an accounting sheet like Microsoft Succeed or research Sheets. QuickBooks and Xero may not be the best fit for your organization. Finding the product that turns out best for your necessities may be the most difficult angle on occasion. We should look into a few accounting software options that can help you get things started. I'll combine Xero with QuickBooks.

Intuit QuickBooks On the web

By far the best bookkeeping and accounting software for independent businesses is QuickBooks Online. It's good that you can link it to your financial condition. This makes it simple to utilize and follow cash when connected to your business account. It makes it simple to accommodate the business account and the books. In spite of the fact that there is something else entirely to QuickBooks On the web.

Only a couple of the highlights inside QuickBooks Online include:

- Cost Invoicing Following
- Stock Control
- Covering Buy Requests

As your organization develops, you might climb to one of the best three levels. This will give you all that you really want for your little business. The accessibility of portable applications for both Android and iOS gadgets is one more astounding element of QuickBooks On the web. The product is likewise viable with most of the outsider projects.

Xero

In the event that you like to deal with a PC or a Macintosh, Xero brings a ton to the table. All that you do in Xero will be went with a video that will help you in learning the program. Xero offers practically identical evaluation and is partitioned into three levels. The fundamental bundle is $12 each month. Coming up next are the qualities of the beginning arrangement:

- Clients are limitless.
- There is a month-to-month furthest reach of five solicitations.
- Breaking point of five bills each month and a limit of twenty exchange compromises consistently

The standard arrangement is $34 each month. This incorporates:

- Clients are limitless.
- Solicitations are limitless.
- Charges Unbounded
- Exchange Compromises are limitless.
- Finance for a limit of five workers

The superior arrangement is $65 each month. Which incorporates:

- Clients are limitless.
- Solicitations are limitless.
- Charges Unbounded
- Exchange Compromises are limitless.
- Finance for a limit of ten workers. Kindly remember that this might be extended to oblige more staff if essential.
- Different monetary standards are upheld. Observe: in the event that you do unfamiliar business, this is a phenomenal element.

Zoho Books

Zoho Books has three cost choices. The most fundamental bundle is $49 each month. This plan just permits you to add 50 contacts and just backings one client. It will permit you to associate with every one of your records and will meet all of your fundamental business needs. On the off chance that you are an independent business visionary, consultant, or Web-based business with a locally established business, this accounting programming is great for you. Different qualities include:

- Exchanges should be accommodated.
- Make Solicitations
- Monitoring Costs
- Project The executives
- Control Time Sheets

The normal bundle costs $99 each month and takes into account two clients. It likewise empowers for the expansion of 500 contacts. This technique incorporates:

- Exchanges should be accommodated.
- Make Solicitations
- Monitoring Costs
- Project The board
- Control Time Sheets
- Screen Bills
- Monitor seller credits.

- Remember Detailing Labels for your Exchanges.

The expert bundle is $249 each month and incorporates 10 clients. This plan likewise incorporates limitless contacts. It likewise contains:

- Exchanges should be accommodated.
- Make Solicitations
- Monitoring Costs
- Project The board

- Control Time Sheets
- Screen Bills
- Monitor seller credits.
- Remember Announcing Labels for your Exchanges.
- Make Deals Requests
- Produce Buy Requests
- Stock Control

Zoho Books gives great client care and backing. The telephones are accessible 24 hours every day, seven days per week. One significant disadvantage of Zoho Books is that it doesn't give finance administrations. This is the greatest option for both you and your company, assuming you have employees.

FreshBooks

With FreshBooks, the estimating depends on dynamic clients. You can find practically every one of the elements in the versatile application that you have on the site. For every one of the plans, you can add project workers at no extra expense. Be that as it may, assuming you really want to add representatives it is an extra $10 each month for every worker.

Representatives can:

- Solicitations and costs might be seen and made.
- Inspect the Dashboard
- Make Reports
- Project workers can:
- View the tasks to which they have been doled out to follow time spent on those ventures.
- Make and send you time-sensitive solicitations.

FreshBooks permits you to make, send and oversee solicitations effectively from your PC or portable application. It additionally takes into consideration quicker installments and makes following your costs simple. With such extraordinary connection points of portable applications, then they additionally have support for those issues that might emerge, too. You will find both telephone and email support, yet it isn't day-in and day-out help.

Wave Bookkeeping

You can likewise add Visa handling for little expense per exchange. This can be added for $35 each month, as well as an extra $6 per representative each month. Wave Bookkeeping is intended for tiny organizations with 10 representatives or fewer and no stock. On the off chance that you anticipate developing your business, ultimately you should progress to one more type of programming.

Month to month Accounting Reports

Commonly, organizations begin to battle since they don't have any idea how the business is doing all along. A decent guideline is to effectively have the books modern and consistently precise. So, I additionally maintain that you should comprehend doing quarterly and yearly reports is similarly as significant. This will assist you with deciding how the organization is doing in general consistently and over time.

Recruit Workers

Adding staff to your organization isn't generally the least demanding thing to do. It involves new commitments, for example, monitoring and paying their compensation. The accounting programming arrangements that we covered before can assist with this. If you have employees, you should make sure the funding option is available. This check is basic to your representatives.

Attempt New Frameworks

There are so many different frameworks that might help your business flourish. We have discussed a couple of the product programs utilized for accounting. In any case, assuming you add an excessive number of frameworks on the double, it very well may be overpowering for you, your workers, and your clients.

Be Involved with your Accountant

Accounting is a fundamental exchange, however, you really do have to see those reports every month, quarter, and year. In the event that you record a receipt or cost in some unacceptable record, the books can in any case adjust however the records may not. Add it to your organization strategy that a standard review will be directed toward the finish of every month or quarter.

Move to a Clerk

In the event that you are the clerk for a drawn-out timeframe, you might need to re-appropriate your accounting. This can be the most financially savvy as you are just paying for several hours of work. In the event that you feel that you can deal with a portion of the accounting and just believe the expert should deal with explicit regions, you can do that too.

One of the benefits of employing an expert is that they can give important business exhort that will assist your organization with growing. A few instances of this exhort incorporate, however, are not restricted to:

- Whether new programming is a good match for your company.
- Go to gatherings with you and your investor.
- Help with yearly spending plans and monetary stream reports
- Train office staff

CHAPTER 5: Generally Accepted Accounting Principles (GAAP)

Bookkeeping requires a comprehension of the regulations or guidelines that administer it. These are otherwise called principles. These standards are in all alluded to as the Proper accounting rules or GAAP.

The guidelines were formulated and created by the Monetary Bookkeeping Establishment's (FAF) standard-setting board. This body is separated into two areas: the Monetary Bookkeeping Principles Board (FASB) and the Legislative Bookkeeping Norms Board (GASB).

These rules oversee the wording utilized in monetary announcing. Thus, it conveys the monetary and functional circumstances. This incorporates companies, both public and private, non-benefit associations, and state or civil legislatures.

Monetary revealing basically remembers data for the accompanying:

- Monetary circumstance (asset report and proclamation of net position)
- Consequences of tasks, which involve income, cost, and net position changes.
- Exposures.

GAAP is utilized to give supportive data to financial backers, banks, and any individual who need to know this data about a firm. It likewise creates ideas, targets, principles, and standards that develop through an opportunity to control how explanations are created and conveyed.

The standards of the GAAP include:

- Acknowledgment involves components like resources, liabilities, pay, and costs that should be kept in a budget summary.
- The parts of the sums that are expressed in the budget reports are alluded to as estimation.
- Show: The details, subtotals, and aggregates are remembered for the fiscal summaries. This is the introduction of that information.
- Divulgence: This offers additional data to oblige the sums on the explanations. Furthermore, it shows particular information as per the client's needs.

Monetary Bookkeeping Establishment (FAF)

- The FAF is an independent, for-benefit organization with its base camp in Norwalk, Connecticut. The Monetary Bookkeeping Guidelines Board and the Legislative Bookkeeping Norms Board are influenced quite a bit by for oversight, the executives, subsidizing, and arrangement.
- The Monetary Bookkeeping Principles Board (FASB) makes bookkeeping and monetary revealing rules for both public and confidential organizations. Similar turns out as expected for philanthropic associations.
- Administrative Bookkeeping Guidelines Board (GASB): They work with bureaucratic, state, and neighborhood legislatures similarly to the FASB does.

The GAAP has forever been a great association of monetary revealing. That way financial backers, moneylenders, capital suppliers, and other people who need admittance to this data can get it. The FASB and GASB are answerable for the GAAP to keep on having those elevated requirements. This cycle empowers board support and will be dependent upon oversight by the FAF's Leading group of Legal administrators.

The FASB and GASB utilize the accompanying strides for fair treatment:

1. Determine Subject: The Board concludes that an issue with monetary revealing must be fixed. This depends on ideas made by closely involved individuals, staff research, board individuals' concerns, or other data.
2. Conduct a Pre-plan study is finished regarding the matters that should be examined.
3. Make a choice with respect to the plan by adding ventures or issues for the public gathering.
4. Discussion at a Public Gathering — A public gathering is met to discuss the issues and stresses.
5. The Board makes a proposition and deliveries it for public conversation. Issue Archive for Public Remark
6. Host Formal reviews or Round Tables (Significant Undertakings) — For significant themes, a formal review might be planned to permit closely involved individuals to voice their viewpoints.
7. Re-intentional A subsequent gathering is coordinated to look at the criticism from the overall population and partners, in view of remarks and exploration.
8. Release of Conclusive Norm — The Board delivers the last report containing the new guidelines.
9. Education: The Board makes sure that everybody is educated about the new necessities.
10. The new necessities have proactively been incorporated.
11. Assuming that it has been set up for a few years and fulfilled the necessary GASB guidelines, then it very well may be chosen for thought for determination by the overseeing body's PPR group.

What are the Characteristics of the GAAP?

All organizations use guidelines in bookkeeping to give data utilized on fiscal reports. The data they need to give is funding, loaning or giving cash, or deciding how public authorities spend our duty dollars. At the point when an organization utilizes fiscal summaries that observe GAAP guidelines then financial backers and others believe that organization.

The House of GAAP

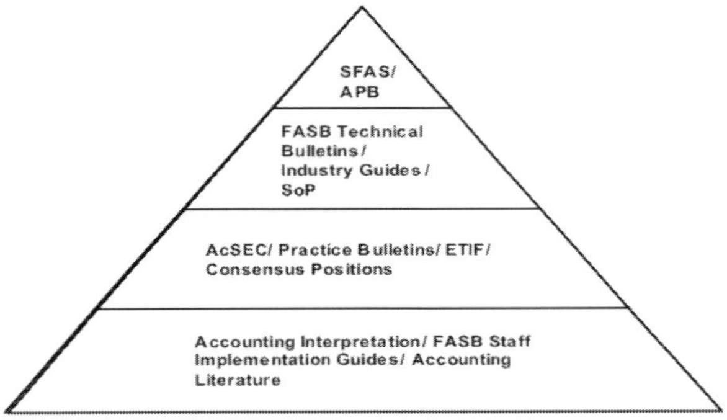

CHAPTER 6:
Types of Financial Statements

The fiscal summaries of an organization are a preview of the strength, execution, and liquidation status of a firm as well as its parent organization. It is required for each organization to make these budget reports toward the finish of each and every financial year. The fiscal reports involve a rundown of the solid, exchanged, and non-performing parts of the organization's tasks. The three principal fiscal summaries are;

Monetary record

The monetary record is an assertion of the monetary place of an association, which shows the monetary remaining of that association at a given time. This assertion is typically ready toward the finish of a bookkeeping period and is arranged to utilize the authentic expense standard.

A sample balance sheet is illustrated in figure 1

Strauss Printing Services
Statement of Financial Position
As of December 31, 2017

ASSETS		
Current Assets:		
Cash	$ 21,000	
Accounts Receivable	16,000	
Prepaid Expenses	4,500	$ 41,500
Non-current Assets:		
Property, Plant and Equipment		145,000
Total Assets		$ 186,500
LIABILITIES AND OWNER'S EQUITY		
Current Liabilities:		
Accounts Payable	$ 8,400	
Rent Payable	8,000	$ 16,400
Non-current Liability:		
Loans Payable		23,000
Strauss, Capital		147,100
Total Liabilities and Owner's Equity		$ 186,500

Figure 1: Illustration of a balance sheet

As you can see, the three elements of accounting are clearly illustrated. There are assets, liabilities, and owner's equity. Note that there are many transactions that occur in a typical company, and the truth is that not all of them are illustrated in the balance sheet. Keep in mind that the balance sheet items only include the three elements of accounting. Therefore, you may want to begin by identifying all of the fixed and current assets, short- and long-term liabilities, and the owner's equity. Ultimately, the figures must balance. In this case, the balancing amount is $186,500

Also, note the manner in which the balance sheet is prepared. The title is always centered and written in three lines. The first line is the name of the company, the second line is an illustration that it is a balance sheet, and the third line is the accounting period. That is the order, and you must always abide by it.

Income statement

The pay proclamation is the part of an organization's business that gives an understanding of the net benefit or deficit made by the organization, as estimated by its investors. It is additionally alluded to as the benefit and misfortune explanation and shows the organization's presentation comparable to its investors' cash.

The contrast between livelihoods can either be positive or negative, where the previous show benefits while the last option demonstrates misfortunes.

An illustration of a profit and loss statement is illustrated in figure 2

Strauss Printing Services
Income Statement
For the Year Ended December 31, 2017

Service Revenue		$ 160,000
Less: Expenses		
Salaries Expense	$ 40,000	
Supplies Expense	26,100	
Rent Expense	20,500	
Utilities Expense	11,300	
Depreciation Expense	5,000	102,900
Net Income		$ 57,100

Figure 2: Illustration of an income statement

Similarly likewise with the accounting report, the heading has three lines. To set up a pay proclamation, remember the accompanying pointers appropriately;

- The expression "benefit and misfortune account" demonstrates that the assertion's essential capability is to determine whether a firm created benefits or misfortunes during a particular time span.
- Take away consumptions from pay to get the last aggregate. An equilibrium that is positive or negative demonstrates a benefit or misfortune.
- Set up the pay articulation consistently using the grouping basis for bookkeeping.

Cash Flow Statement

The income proclamation sums up the progression of endlessly cash same and shows the development of money over a predefined timeframe. The term cash signifies "like," and that amounts to something that can measure up to cash. A few well-known instances of endlessly cash comparable are:

- Stocks
- Certificates of deposit
- Shares

At the point when you have recognized all of your endless cash reciprocals, you can continue to set up a budget summary - here you list your resources and liabilities as well as your current and non-current liabilities.

Operating, investing, and financing operations are the statement's main components.

- Working exercises are income age exercises that incorporate exercises like the deal and acquisition of labor and products. For example, on the off chance that you have a shirt-selling shop, the working exercises will rotate around purchasing natural substances and selling the shirts on either a money or credit premise. These are the principal processes that act as fundamental income-creating processes.
- Contributing exercises are those exercises that have the goal of creating pay from now on, like the buy and offer of long-haul resources. Many organizations don't just work inside themselves, and they purchase stocks and offers from different organizations to expand their security.

- Income from working exercises is the development of money for the sole motivation behind funding the organization all's business activities.

Some of the minor accounts include the statement of shareholders' equity as well as general reports.

CHAPTER 7:
The Accounting Cycle and the Closing Process

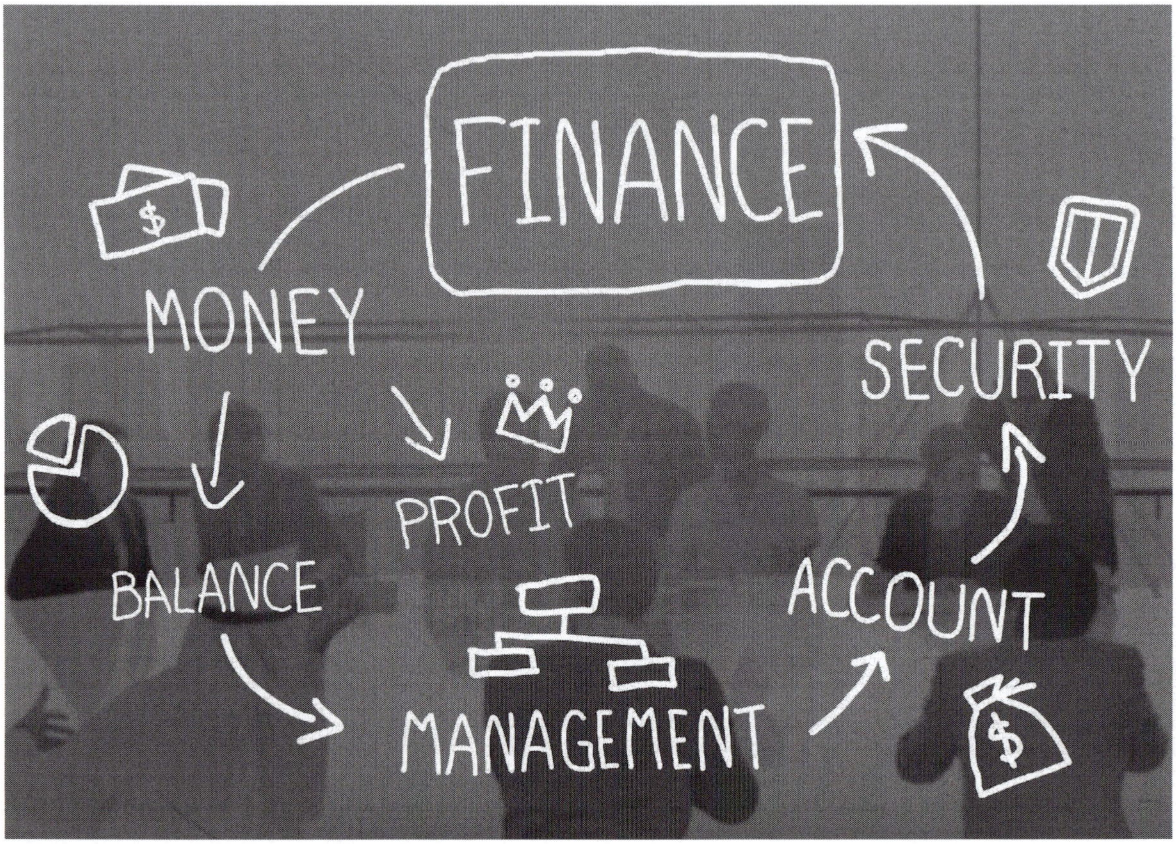

Budget summaries give a 10,000-foot view of how a business is doing. A business might record hundreds, even thousands, of monetary exchanges throughout a year. Fiscal reports are ready, to sum up the impact of point-by-point monetary exchanges. The bookkeeping cycle depicts common exercises a business goes through during its bookkeeping period.

The phases of the bookkeeping cycle

1. Transactions

Trades: Monetary trades put the cycle into high gear. Assuming there were no monetary exchanges, there would not be anything to watch. Trades may be the result of a commitment, any buys or benefits acquired, income from deals, or any costs made.

2. Journal Sections

Sections in the Association's Diary: After the trades have been made, the accompanying step is to keep these passages in the association's journal sequentially. While charging something like one record and crediting somewhere around one record, changes ought to be made reliably.

3. Posting to the Overall Record (GL)

The diary segments are then given on the general record, which likewise records any correspondence to explicit records.

4. Trial Equilibrium

Preliminary Equilibrium: A total balance of the records is laid out after the bookkeeping time span, which might be quarterly, month to month, or yearly, contingent upon the organization.

5. Worksheet

Worksheet: The representative should explore slip-ups and make rectifications that are reported on a worksheet when the charges and credits on the preliminary equilibrium don't coordinate.

6. Adjusting Sections

Changes in Sections: At the finish of the association's accounting time frame, changes in passages for gatherings and deferrals should be submitted.

7. Financial Proclamations

Monetary synopses: With the legitimate changes, the resource report, pay clarification, and pay enunciation may be in every way created.

8. Closing

End: The income and company records are done and ready for the impending accounting cycle. This is so execution for a specific time frame might be found in the compensation decree accounts that are pay and company records. Since they portray the association's monetary condition at one point in time, financial record accounts are not shut.

Accounting Cycle – General Ledger

Each monetary exchange that happens inside a firm is kept in the general record, which goes about as the representatives' and clerks' eyes and ears. Fundamentally, the current strategy is a huge collection of all exchanges recorded on a specific report or on bookkeeping programming. For example, you would check the general record, which records every one of the charges and credits of cash, assuming you expected to see how genuine cash levels altered during the direction of the business and all their significant trades.

Accounting Cycle Fundamentals

To totally comprehend the bookkeeping cycle, one priority is a solid handle of the key bookkeeping rules. Contemplate the coordination standard, the gathering rule, and income acknowledgment (the place where an organization might record bargain pay).

You can deliver the main stages in the bookkeeping cycle — the pay enunciation, resource report, and pay clarification — by utilizing these essential thoughts. View the free Bookkeeping Basics Course presented by CFI to find out more.

The methodology used to set up for the finish of the spending plan report and the start of the resulting bookkeeping period is known as the bookkeeping finishing process, frequently known as shutting the books. The last stage includes establishing the general record for the impending bookkeeping time frame and moving brief record corrections to extremely durable standards.

The records of an organization's monetary exercises are known as "the books." The data is utilized to deliver reports that exhibit to entrepreneurs how much cash is traveling through their undertaking.

The end of the books connotes that these reports are done. These completed reports show an organization's monetary situation all through a specific bookkeeping period, which may be a month or a year.

The importance of the closing process

The last step is to ensure that no compensation or expenses from the earlier bookkeeping time frame are extended to the ongoing bookkeeping time frame and slant its outcomes.

Consistently, associations close their books so they can produce monetary reports that show proprietors how their organization is doing monetarily. At year's end, free endeavors regularly give declarations like a resource report and a compensation clarification to assess what is happening as they make arrangements for the impending year.

To accurately report their yearly government desk work, entrepreneurs should close their records toward the year's end. Accurately shutting the books additionally ensures that your bookkeeping framework is functional and that it is creating exact numbers for you to record on your consumption structure.

The end of the books consistently is likewise standard. Month-to-month exercises like refreshing your ledger, sending bargains charge reports to the state, paying your providers, and composing client clarifications are made simpler with this methodology.

CHAPTER 8: Major Types of Businesses

In the bookkeeping domain, the legitimate design might direct the way that things ought to be finished. For instance, not a wide range of organizations grant the proprietor to pull out assets from the organization. Accounting depends on normal standards in regards to the importance of fiscal summaries, which vary for the benefit and non-benefit substances. As a clerk or bookkeeper, you ought to know about this.

What differentiates various types of business?

- Expenses of organizations: Some businesses sorts are absolved from tax collection or pay less duty than others.
- Deciding: Contingent upon the kind of business, choices are made in various ways.

- Contingent upon the kind of business, various sums are expected to send off and enroll it.
- A few organizations are easy to enroll and send off, however, others are seriously difficult.
- Contingent upon how a firm is organized, different monetary dangers might be available.

These are the business categories that are most common:

Sole proprietorship

Sole ownership isn't just the most widely recognized sort of business, yet it is additionally the most established. The proprietor accepts all business dangers and obligations - he completely funds the business and partakes in the advantages all alone. Contingent upon the proprietor's pioneering abilities and monetary establishment, a sole ownership business can develop into a uber business.

Partnership

An association is a business that is possessed by at least two individuals - the greatest number of accomplices can vary by country. The accomplices are the entrepreneurs, and they go with joint choices to run it. A bookkeeper will set up allotment records to follow capital commitments and withdrawals from accomplices. An organization's understanding ought to basically incorporate the accompanying:

- Portray the sort of business the accomplices intend to work and how the financing will be given.
- Make sense of the appropriation of benefit and misfortune.
- As to an accomplice who might get paid from the business
- How could questions be taken care of

Partnerships are usually registered under the company act in most countries and form part of the UK's Business Corporations register.

Limited company

A restricted organization's capital is contributed by its investors, however, the organization's liabilities are restricted. Its lawful construction is particular and unmistakable from its proprietors. Private or public restricted organizations can be framed. A restricted organization is a business that is possessed by at least one person.

There are two types of limited companies:

Private limited companies

This is an organization that is claimed by confidential investors. Confidential restricted partnerships can likewise be partitioned into two classifications:

Confidential restricted organization with an offer-based capital

Confidential restricted business with a restricted obligation contract

Public limited company (PLC)

The difference between a public company and a private limited company (PLC) is that the PLC's portions can be claimed, sold, and proposed to people in general. PLCs are more difficult to set up and enlist than private restricted organizations. They can also be recorded on a stock exchange, allowing the population to exchange with them.

Cooperative

A group of people coming together to work toward a common goal is useful. Ranchers, for example, may band together with the goal of improving their product and marketing it. Individuals from a helpful choose an administration council to direct their everyday tasks. The normal reason basically tries to help agreeable individuals monetarily and instructively.

CHAPTER 9:
Forensic accounting

Legal bookkeeping is the bookkeeping specialty practice region that researches whether firms participate in monetary revealing misrepresentation. Scientific bookkeepers utilize different abilities and strategies to decide if monetary revealing extortion has happened.

Most Common Fraud Schemes

One of the most challenging aspects is the millions of fraud cases that are out there. This is a decent spot to begin as most cases start or end with one of these.

Skimming

It is when an employee asks for slightly more than what the business is asking – for a product or service – and pockets the extra. It is common with professional practices which accept fees paid in cash. For example, a cashier who takes in cash and does not record it in the accounting record. Or maybe they did, but the transaction was deliberately deleted.

Write-Offs that are Fraudulent or Lapping

False discounts or lapping can be set aside via sorting room workers who installment installments into their own ledgers rather than the organization's record. At the point when there is no concealment, the plan is thwarted rapidly - the organization will send a subsequent notification or bill to the client expressing that the bill is late. This kind of extortion can be concealed by the client giving a duplicate of the dropped check.

Using Shell Companies

Higher management or employees typically create shell companies to sell fictitious services and goods. The person who owns the shell company will sign off on the disbursement to the company they work for. Shell company bills, however, are missing one key element – authenticity. Each bill has the company's address, but it is the same address as a supervisor at the company.

Any time you are working for a company, it is important to check their list of vendors and get verification.

Creating Ghost Employees

Phantom representatives is a false plan normal among chiefs of HR and Finance. These two regions are in the situation to make and delete representatives who don't "in fact" work for the organization. These workers are then added to the finance and faculty records and in this manner get a "regularly scheduled check". Apparition representatives are hazardous for organizations as they cost them tremendous measures of cash.

This kind of extortion is the hardest to identify. When a phantom representative is made, it seems to be some other worker account-wise. A few regions to check are days off, excursion days, work execution, and so on, as phantom representatives don't "as a matter of fact" work for the organization. In the event that there is still misrepresentation, however, it appears in different data sets, a few representatives may be cooperating to share the unlawful benefits.

Shrinkage of Inventory

When a business sells products, there is usually a sales and inventory account that is affected. Granted, when a person steals the inventory, the sale isn't recorded, and thus there is a decrease in inventory. Whenever a business has inventory, it will have some shrinkage due to normal business operations. It is the unusual shrinkage that causes the concerns and red flags.

An investigation may show a fraud scheme when all items within a business's inventory are affected by the same amount of shrinkage at the same time. Any time there is a normal shrinkage or an event that causes it, all items in the business are affected. When there is no trend or pattern for inventory shrinkage, then an investigation may indicate something is amiss.

Management Embezzlement

This can occur in any association - little or enormous, corporate or military.

How about we check out the case of Tyco Global. They had three top officials who were accused of stealing funds. The association's chief was one of these authorities. Because of their status inside the organization, they could excuse credits to one another - in this way they were taking from the organization. When gotten, they were charged for the robbery of >$170,000,000 of organization credits.

Security Fraud

You have probably noticed the tighter restrictions with banks. This was caused by the series of financial collapses that occurred after the global recession. Security fraud is a serious crime. Typically, it is committed by an entire brokerage firm or an individual. One way to combat such fraud is to hire a forensic accountant. They will thoroughly look through the financial statements for clues that will support any claims of fraud.

A forensic accountant will investigate the company to see if there is any evidence of security fraud or insider trading, for example. There are several ways security fraud can occur:

Misrepresentation of information in the SEC filing

Companies who are publicly traded file SEC reports. An investor will typically use these reports to help determine if this company will be a good investment. If this information is filed with misleading information about the company's performance and assets, a crime has been committed. In turn, this could lead to civil charges and litigation of the company.

An investigation happens when there is a suspicion of security fraud. One thing that is looked at in-depth is the financial statements. If there is any security fraud, it may be possible that there will be a history of it somewhere within the records of the business.

Performing account fraud

After the downturn, the Dodd-Forthright Money Road Change, and Buyer Insurance Act were presented. This act was made to change the monetary guidelines and increment straightforwardness. What is deterring is the manner by which organizations come up short at an endeavor or have taken a speculation risk that didn't pay off, and afterward, attempt to conceal the obligations and misfortunes.

A scientific bookkeeper has immense information about what the security guidelines and the Sound accounting standards (GAAP) mean for an organization. With this information, they can go through an organization's records and track down the secret misfortunes to choose if the firm was giving financial backers deluding data.

Engaging in a form of insider trading

Insider trading is when someone knows something that could affect the value of a company's assets or stock. What if they knew the company was seeing the dangers of bankruptcy? They could then try to sell this information to investors of the company. This would be a great temptation to use to invest in the company, such as insider trading.

Putting money toward a scam or another form of hedge fund

Using the money that is for investors and misappropriating a fund is fraud. This is where hedge funds come in - stolen money from a parent fund is deposited into these "hedge funds" instead. This means that the investor gave money and expected a specific return, but instead, the money was used for something else.

Forensic Accounting Methods

Tracing money is a tedious job and can take days or months to find the source and crack the case. Forensic accounting is about investigating the clues and following the trail. Sometimes this is as easy as checking bank records or as hard as needed to investigate one back to another, as the money is floated until its final destination.

Take an example of an employee wiring money from a company account to their personal account, and it will stay in this dummy account for a few days before being transferred to another dummy account. It could easily follow this pattern for months before it gets to the intended account for the employee who stole the money. Keep in mind that even this account may be a dummy, and they can access it through other means.

An employee who steals $10,000 and moves it from one bank to another using very small amounts may end up with $9,500 that has already been deposited into their real account. This makes it harder to detect and will not raise red flags with their bank. It is a great challenge to find money and catch up to it as the money is floated between banks.

A logical bookkeeper locks onto the cash trail and begins to see every one of the banks it has gone through. They then, at that point, explore every one of those records and figure out that a limited quantity has been removed each time. Did the false worker utilize a card and pull out the cash? Assuming this is the case, was it in a similar area each time? Was it inside a similar city or state? At the point when the worker utilizes an ATM card, it is recorded.

A scientific bookkeeper must be so familiar with the representatives and employees that people mistake them for the leader or the president. They will start by asking queries such as, "What kind of person is every person?" These straightforward questions will provide the bookkeeper with a list of potential candidates to start thinking about.

A forensic accountant is someone who has to be organized, organized and have knowledge of computer programs like Word, Excel, and Access to help investigators with their investigations. Today, most records are electronic and easier to request, and it does not take as long to get the records, and the investigation will not stop because of the records.

The Records

A forensic accountant will look at e-mails, databases, ledgers, journals, credit statements, bank statements, etc. as part of their work for a police or criminal investigation.

A forensic accountant is a detective and thus must suspect everyone. Once they have all the records in order, it is time for interviews. These interviews are not only with the employees the records indicate to, but also with anyone who knows information about the case. If someone has access to the records, they need to be interviewed.

As the interviews are conducted, the interviewees' behaviors are observed for clues. They are not going to tell the truth – even though that would make the case easier to solve – so the accountant must look for clues about them taking several vacations or purchasing things like a new car. For example, if an employee is only on a minimum wage and has a family of five, the odds are that they cannot afford to go on several vacations or a brand-new car. Truly, this by itself doesn't say made them fake, so further assessment of their funds is required. Perhaps they have one more work and type of revenue? All of this data helps fabricate the master plan.

The context of the case will depend on how far a forensic accountant needs to look for information. When the case is of a criminal nature, then they work with the district attorney's office and law enforcement.

A search warrant or subpoena must be obtained to obtain personal and financial records from companies and individuals in a criminal investigation. It is important to know that companies and banks have client and employee confidentiality agreements. This means they cannot give this information to anyone except the client or employee – unless there is a signed document by them stating otherwise.

Now that forensic accountant has gathered all the evidence, they need to analyze it. This may require a trace of all the assets the company has, calculation of the total losses, documenting how the theft occurred, and summarizing the various transactions. The report must be thorough and include spreadsheets, charts, and graphs. A good rule of thumb is to add an in-depth summary of findings and include all organized notes in the report as supporting evidence.

Indirect and Direct Methods

The direct method involves looking at all public records, agreements, contracts, invoices, and canceled checks. There may also be interviews with the employees and management. The indirect method is based on the bank deposit method and the net worth method.

The Net Worth Method

An investigation may go in several directions depending on if there are unreconciled differences between a company's assets and liabilities. This method calculates the company or individual's total assets and then subtracts the total liabilities. The aftereffect of this estimation is the total assets, which is then looked at over numerous periods.

The Bank Deposit Method

Through this method, total deposits made during the year are analyzed and then compared with the total expenses. If there are any transfers between accounts, they are subtracted from the total deposits for that year to arrive at the net deposits. The total expenditures for that year will be added to the net deposits to give a total receipt for the year. This number will be compared to the funds from any known sources which will determine the total amount of funds from the unknown sources. The forensic accountant will now start to investigate the unknown sources. This investigation may include searching or tracking information for the specific amount in question. It may also require them to interview key individuals as they come up in the investigation.

All these methods are essential to an investigation and will bring the detective closer to finding the truth.

Technology and Tools Used

We live in a digital age of computers and technology. Granted, as life advances, so do crimes. Now, we are faced with digital crime, and our techniques and tools need to be upgraded to keep up with it.

Financial fraud is simpler to perpetrate thanks to technology. Most companies have all their financials online through "cloud" technology, and this can be placed into two categories: tool or target.

The following are a few examples of such tools:

Helix

This is a great Internet tool that is used to collect sound images from several different types of drives. This also includes partition drives that use a unique system setup like RAID arrays. Several systems offer the same service; however, this system is different as it is free and open source.

Helix can be utilized as a criminological boot with x86 frameworks or as a live scientific picture. At the point when a PC is closed down, there is a decent opportunity that proof could be obliterated. Subsequently, a scientific inspector should be cautious while closing down a PC. The most effective way to close down the PC, without gambling with the deficiency of information, is by turning off it. Helix goes through the Linux side, and the framework can be rebooted utilizing Helix. When this happens, it will show the work area with everything as a read-as it was. This will keep the information from being changed in any capacity.

Leg tendon Desktop

This framework characterizes ACL as a helpful device that will likewise understand well and dissect records. These documents might be dissipated through a few data sets all through various stages. It will give a prompt visual of information that is basic for an association. This will permit investigation of the relative multitude of information that is populated for complete confirmation.

UltraBlock

UltraBlock is a legal compose blocker equipment framework. It makes it unimaginable for information to be changed. It is additionally viable with different apparatuses. In any case, it is additionally costly and extremely difficult to maintain up-to-date reports and records.

Passware Kit Forensic

This is a great tool that is used for the discovery of evidence reports that are password-protected on the computer that is being investigated. It will give access to items by using one of the fastest password and decryption recovery algorithms. This will allow the recovery of the strongest passwords.

These are all great tools; however, they do not replace hard evidence and documents from outside sources. Anything that is obtained through these tools must be checked for authenticity.

Lessons Learned

Forensic accounting has been around for centuries and has helped in some of the most prominent legal cases to date. Let's look back on some and see what made each case success or a failure.

1. *The Enron Scandal*

This scandal is the most prominent case in American history and took place between the mid-1980s and 2001. Millions of dollars were hidden through projects that had failed and raked up debt. The scandal involved company executives and the accounting team working together to hide the money.

Enron had a creative team of accountants with skilled techniques. They worked hard to hide debt in the partnerships, misrepresent the money on the financial statements, and inflate the debt ratings and price stocks.

Through the demonstrations of these pioneers, the stock cost for Enron crashed. It was at $90 per share and promptly dropped to $1 per share. This raised an enormous warning for the organization. An examination started where a legal bookkeeper uncovered a great deal of stowed away data. The CEO, Jeff Skilling, was accused of a few crimes and served fourteen years in jail. The previous CEO, Kenneth Lay, was tracked down liable on ten counts of safety extortion. He died prior to being shipped off jail.

2. *The AIG Scandal*

The fraud with the American International Group, Inc went from December 2000 to March 2001. AIG entered a series of transactions with Gen Re Corporation that were fraudulent. The purpose was to create a reinsurance policy that was false. This was to increase the appearance of AIG loss reserves and a report on the balance sheet to reflect that.

The investigation was at both the state and federal levels. Forensic experts were on the trail for clues and eventually found the fraudulent transactions. Through an SEC investigation and a trial, AIG was guilty of accounting fraud. AIG was defrauding its analysts and investors. They also violated the policies set by the SEC and the GAAP.

AIG was fined $100,000,000. They also needed to make it right to their investors and were required to give $700,000,000 of their gains back to their investors.

CHAPTER 10:
Payroll

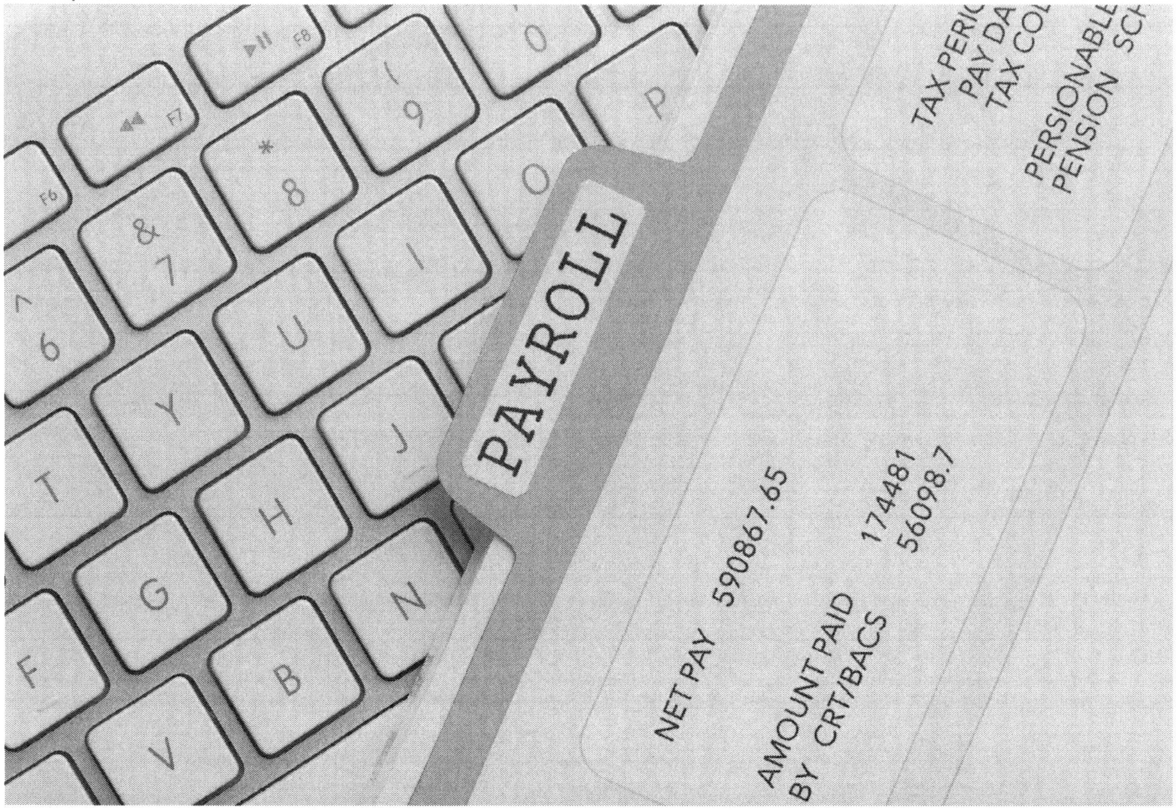

The term payroll usually refers to the amount of money paid out to employees per pay period. Payrolls may take into account deductions for tax, federal and state benefits, and other payroll taxes.

If your company pays its employees on a monthly basis, then this is known as an "hourly" or "salaried" system. The amount of money you pay your employees for each pay period is based on the total number of hours worked. Both systems use the same payroll procedures.

Payroll procedures are designed to calculate the correct amount of money that should be paid to each employee in each pay period. There are two types of payroll procedures - there are two different ways of calculating this - one is a manual process and the other is a computerized one.

Organizations utilizing more than one representative normally utilize a "finance" framework, which pays every worker a foreordained pay consistently no matter what the number of hours worked. This framework is otherwise called an "excluded" framework since it can satisfy government Fair Labor Standards Act exclusion prerequisites if appropriately kept up with and made due. The government propels organizations to pay all non-excluded representatives basically the bureaucratic, the lowest pay permitted by law for every hour worked.

Items for payroll and benefits

The following items and benefits will be included in the payroll:

- Salaries & Wages
- Commissions and incentives for employees
- Compensation for overtime

Payroll taxes and expenses

- Security benefits
- Tax on unemployment
- Social Security tax
- Insurance for workers' compensation

Employer-provided benefits

- Coverage for Travel (health, dental, vision, life, disability)
- strategies for sharing profits
- Retirement preparations
- Sick time Holidays

Assuming there is no immediate connection among incomes and costs, the cost ought to be recorded on the pay articulation for the bookkeeping time frame in which it was brought about. An organization should match its costs to the bookkeeping time frames in which the connected incomes are accounted for. Most of these things are represented by public regulations however they cannot be entirely set in stone by organizations' own strategies and practices.

Cash Method

The cash method is an accounting method that recognizes revenue (income) in the period when the cash is received and expenses (expenses) during the period of time when the money is paid.

If a company sends an invoice to a customer, it will not be counted as sales until the customer's cash is reflected in their account. If the company receives bills, such as electricity bills, the expense won't be recognized until the bills are actually paid.

Accrual method

The company uses the accrual method - a method of accounting that records revenue (income) in the period earned and expenses incurred - rather than the period they are incurred.

A company will record sales revenue even if cash has not yet been deposited into their bank account if they have sent an invoice to a customer. For example, if a company delivers services or products and sends an invoice, the customer's bank account will be charged even if no cash has been deposited yet.

Accounting using the accrual method (basis) is more formal and accurate. It is the one used to record transactions by both private and public formal entities. If a company receives bills, such as electricity bills, the expenses are recorded even if the company has yet to commit cash to offset the expense.

Matching principles real-life scenarios

Scenario 1

ABC hires Miss Senaah Buria for a week from April 23 to April 30. On April 30, Senaah submits her time card for payment. The company issues her with a payroll check of $140 dated May 5 the immediate date on which the company makes payments.

Even though the check is dated May 5, the matching principle directs that the $140 payroll expense be recorded in April as an expense on the payroll expense account and a current liability on payroll liability accounts; this is the time when Miss Senaah Buria performed the work she being paid for on

May 5. Since Senaah was only employed for a week, ABC will not have payroll expenses in May. On May 5 when the payment is actually affected, will only offset the corresponding liability account.

Scenario 2

ABC signs a contract with Mr. Alex Maunda the sales executive for one the year of 2017 from Jan 1 to Dec 31. The agreement states that the sales manager will be paid a 2% bonus of total sales that occurred in the year 2017 from Jan to Dec. The bonuses will be paid once on Jan 10 of 2018.

ABC made the following sales during the year 2017

Month	Sales ($)	Monthly Bonuses 2% of monthly sales ($)
Jan	15,000	300
Feb	17,000	340
Mar	15,500	310
Apr	19,000	380
May	17,800	356
Jun	19,500	390
Jul	21,200	424
Aug	22,000	440
Sept	25,000	500
Oct	26,000	520
Nov	27,500	550
Dec	28,300	566
Total Sales	**253,800**	**5,076**

According to the sales statement of 2017 presented in the table, Mr. Maunda is paid 2% of $253,800. The bonus is actually paid in 2018. The matching principle requires that the bonuses are expensed alongside the period sales occurred. It will be recorded as liabilities which will be offset in 2018 when the payment is made.

If ABC ignores bonus expenses in 2017 and decide to record the expense once on Jan 10 of 2018 when the payment for the bonuses is made, the income statement of 2017 will record more net income because the bonus expenses which occurred to generate the listed revenue in the statement have been postponed to another reporting period. On the other hand, the income statement of 2018 will record little net income because is expensed with bonus expenses from the previous period.

In this scenario, the correct reporting would be to report bonus expenses for the period of time in which the bonus was paid rather than the amount owed. Debit the payroll account available for handling bonuses appropriately and then credit the liability account.

Sales are recorded as part of the income statement, rather than the current financial year, so the liability account will be debited when the payment is actually made in January 2018. The liability amount will reflect in the 2017 balance sheet in which the sales are reported to HM Revenue and Customs.

Salaries

Payments to employees can be made once a month, semi-monthly (in the middle of the month), every two weeks, or as directed by the company's salary policy. Salaried employees are more likely to receive a fixed amount at the end of a fixed period (month) regardless of the amount of service provided by the employee. Employees are paid per hour, not per minute, and their pay will vary according to the number of hours worked. Wages are calculated using time metrics and a rate per unit of time - if an employee works more than 20 hours a week, for example, they may be paid per minute rather than hourly.

Wages

The term "gross wage" describes an employee's compensation before any deductions, such as those made for taxes. If the worker receives any additional compensation, it should be added to the base pay. Depending on the kind of organization, the gross compensation amount may change from pay period to pay period.

Employees' Bonuses and Commissions

Bonuses and sales commissions should be recognized and recorded during the sales period. Employee bonuses and commissions will be considered part of their gross salary.

pay for overtime

More than 40 hours a week of labor is considered overtime. Company policies and employee work obligations affect overtime pay. C-level executives and other staff are excluded from overtime compensation. This indicates that they are not owed overtime compensation by their employers. This is because of the following factors:

1. They can control their working hours because they have the authority to do so. They do not require labor laws to protect themselves; they can protect themselves by controlling their work hours and working extra hours as they see fit.
2. Their compensation is high.

Overtime Premium

Overtime premium is used to calculate the hourly rate for overtime hours. For example, an employee who is paid $15 per hour worked for 45 hours in a week. This represents 5 hours of overtime. The regular hour's pay of the week is computed by multiplying 40 hours by an hourly rate of $15. (40 x15) =$600. The extra 5 hours are overtime and are paid at the rate of $15 + (15/2) = $22.5

Overtime premium = 5 hours x 22.5 per hour = 112.5

Total weekly wage gross amount = Regular hours wage + overtime premium ($600+$112.5) = $712.5

Payroll Withholdings

Payroll taxes are not taken from employees' gross wages; instead, employee taxes and perks are. The deductions from employees' gross pay are the subject of this section of payroll accounting. Payroll taxes, however, are taken from an employee's final income rather than being withheld from their gross pay.

Examples of general payroll withholdings:

1. Employee's share of Social Security contributions
2. Employee share of medical tax
3. Income taxation at the national or federal level
4. Court-ordered withholding
5. Income taxation
6. Other deductions

Employee social security tax

The Social Security tax is deducted from employee paychecks, and both the employer and employee are responsible for paying it. In other nations, it may go by different names.

Employee share of medical tax

Medical tax is a type of social security withholding that is subtracted from an employee's pay, and both the employer and employee are responsible for paying healthcare tax. The business is expected to transmit both the representative and boss portions of the clinical duty to the suitable organization charge body.

Income tax

is another part of payroll accounting. Employers must withhold the income tax that employees are obligated to pay depending on their incomes or earnings. The actual amount owing for the year will be determined by the employee's year-end income tax return, meaning that the employee would either pay higher taxes or receive a tax refund.

The figure is based on a range of factors including pay, compensation, and personal information submitted to the employer.

CHAPTER 11: Planning and Budgeting

A budget is a plan of what we want to spend our money on and how much we need to set aside in order to make the goal happen. Planning is a positive development, however it's not the last word. A spending plan ought to be surveyed consistently, adjusted if important and refreshed as funds change with the goal that you have a more exact perspective on your life and your business' monetary circumstance. So many people fail without even starting out because they don't realize that plans change and start looking at their budget from this angle. There are also many aspects that often go unexplained such as taxes, growth projections, cash flow etc...

Your budget is the engine that helps you plan and manage your cash. A budget is a list of the things you want and need, ranked in order of importance, with money allocated to each one. Budgeting means deciding ahead how much of your money to give to each item on the list. Planning means looking at your finances and deciding where you want to spend and save your money right now.

Planning can help reduce stress because it's taking control over how much money you have coming in, as well as what money will be spent at this point in time. If you spend your money wisely, you'll be able to save more for the future.

Spending plans can be exceptionally helpful for settling on conclusions about purchasing things that your business needs — or needs. Settling what you need to purchase and its amount is a difficult decision. Assuming that you're arranging, you can choose if you truly need this thing, or on the other hand assuming it would simply bring "allurement" into your life as profound ups and downs! If so, then, at that point, don't get it at the present time.

You can also use a budget to decide if you need to cut back. See if you can do something that doesn't bring any joy or excitement into your life, but will help make ends meet.

Budgets help you decide how much of the revenue generated needs to be spent right now and how much is left over for saving and investing.

Purpose of planning and budgeting.

It is the process of working out how you intend to achieve your goals or satisfy your targets. This often starts with assessing the resource needs of a business. It is vital for successful management, as it ensures that the company has sufficient capital for long-term operations, makes sound investment decisions, and does not commit any resources unnecessarily. In addition, planning and budgeting help to ensure that resources are allocated equitably across projects or activities, which can help avoid conflicts among different teams of employees who share similar goals but have different resources available to them.

The preparation and planning cycle. The preparation and planning cycle includes seven particular advances. These means should be applied in a consecutive request.

1. Clarifying the goal or objective with a vision statement, mission statement, or similar statement that outlines what the business wants to be for its employees, customers, investors, regulators, or other key stakeholders, including government agencies and investors. This is an

inspirational message that ensures that everyone in the business understands where it's heading and what it's trying to achieve. The purpose is to make sure everybody understands why the business exists and what its major functions are all about.

2. Clearly define the key KPIs / objectives of the business, with a response to the following questions:
    - What drives the business?
    - What is its vision of where it expects to be in three years' time?
    - What are its main achievements, both past, and future?
    - Are there any new processes or systems that need to be introduced?
    - Do we need to review our cost base, organically or through acquisitions and new businesses?
3. Sales organizations need to make a list of key objectives for the year ahead, which could include financial performance, staff numbers, changes in product mix, service levels, number of sales calls per month (SPC), and cost-effectiveness. Identifying goals and targets that would help achieve these objectives is one of the most important elements of a company's strategy.
4. Allocating specific tasks to achieve these goals, or recording how these goals would be achieved (e.g., by identifying specific products, services, or procedures.)
5. Estimating how much time and/or money will be required to achieve the goals. This can also be called budgeting or forecasting, including a review of any financial implications such as:
    - Impact on cash flow from sales is greater than anticipated; higher levels of expenditure forecast than are expected to come in from sales; and potential cash flow problems that might arise. It could include an analysis of the implications of different interest rates on any borrowing required by the business.
6. Creating a detailed plan for achieving these goals with an evaluation of the costs, time, and risks involved. This could include an analysis of the implications of different interest rates on any borrowing required by the business.

7. Evaluating results against plan and prior to making any changes that may have a significant impact on long-term plans or strategies.

Strengths and weaknesses of planning and budgeting

Strengths of planning and budgeting:

- A process for getting everybody to work together toward common goals
- A systematic way of delivering on annual goals
- A method for identifying resource needs that can be used to help allocate resources appropriately
- Identification of the strategies required to achieve the long-term objectives or to reach the long-term objectives proposed in the strategic plan
- An opportunity to review the performance of individual roles or groups against targets, with a view to taking corrective action if necessary. In particular, it reminds managers that they should keep honest financial records. It helps firms avoid overstating profits, which could lead investors to make inappropriate decisions.

CHAPTER 12: Bookkeeping tips for your Small Business

With just the right amount of arranging, you can have your records exact and finished consistently. I need to require a couple of moments to go through more than a couple of tips that you can follow. These tips won't just make things simpler for you, as the entrepreneur, yet in addition your accountant.

Tip 1: Maintain Correct Records

Web-based financial will simplify it to follow charges and credits, however it doesn't mean you don't require accounting records. This following methodology will be made more straightforward by making a savvy interest in real money premise bookkeeping programming. The main viewpoint is that your monetary records are undeniably kept in one spot.

Tip 2: Sort and File Receipts

In your business, you will have a lot of receipts on a daily or monthly basis. Over time the ink on the receipts will fade. It can be good to photocopy or scan your receipts. Then arrange them according to chronology so that they correlate with your thorough financial records.

Tip 3: Collect Applicable Taxes

You really want to gather or apply charges when they happen, for example, when a deal is made or finance is produced. Very much like with the receipts, the more you go between the exchanges, the more opportunities for blunders. Make certain to deal with the assessments when they happen. This will ensure that your organization will not owe a lot of duties at the same time toward the year's end or have to deal with damages for making late expense installments.

Tip 4: Make appropriate billing.

Giving your customers an invoice will inform them of the amount and due date for payments. Receipts are your company's costs or cash outflows; think of them as potential future cash inflows. The terms "invoice" and "receipt" refer to two separate types of payment, not the same thing.

Tip 5: Get Donation and Contribution Receipts

Making a contribution has tax advantages, but you'll need a receipt as proof of your generosity. Each receipt must state the donation's value in terms of American tax law. A check alone won't suffice to verify the legitimacy of some gifts.

Tip 6: Schedule Profit and Loss Statements

Profit and Loss. Statements are a great way to check the health of your company. You can have a P&L scheduled monthly, quarterly, or annually. It can provide an overview of many areas of the business for a given period.

Personal and Financial Records (P&L) are important pieces of paper that you keep for your business. Your bookkeeper or accountant may find discrepancies in the P&L as each one is pulled. It is important to have these printed to give them an idea of which period of time that discrepancy occurred so that it can be corrected.

The simplest chores often turn out to be the most crucial. If you stick to a regular schedule of chores, it will be simpler to complete each of these activities. Create a calendar to serve as a reminder of the tasks you need to do, their due dates, and the amount of time required for each.

Keep your business records accurate and organized on a daily basis. This will eliminate so much frustration along the way. Most of that scary feeling and large bit of time comes from poor preparation, especially in bookkeeping and accounting. Proper time management is the key ingredient for success.

FINAL WORDS

This book has given you the tools to better understand not only your bookkeeper, but also your business and how to run a successful company from a bookkeeper's point of view as well as a business owner's perspective on finances and accounts receivables.

"It is not the business owner that runs the business, it is the business owners teamed up with the bookkeeper," says Dr. Sears. Each area that we have covered in this article has a purpose and when you work hand-in-hand with your bookkeeper, you will see the light at the end of the tunnel.

The bookkeeper is the gatekeeper for your business. They hold the power over the financial health of your business and ensure that all transactions are made in accordance with the laws of England and Wales, as well as keeping you up-to-date on your company's finances.

I've given you the authority to hold yourself to the same standard as your accountant and bookkeeper. You can do anything as a group. Your bookkeeper can make sure you have all you need to steer your company in the proper way. They may also aid you in making the appropriate choices. If the trend is stable, you can anticipate the future with the right analysis and ratios.

This is an excellent place to begin whether you are considering starting a business or are already in the process of doing so. Additionally, you'll be more equipped to include your financial information in your company plan and pitch deck. I am forward to seeing your company operating and learning about the fantastic success you will be experiencing.